2018 SQA Specimen and Past Papers with Answers

Higher
COMPUTING SCIENCE

2017 & 2018 Exams
and 2018 Specimen Question Paper

Hodder Gibson Study Skills Advice –
   Higher Computing Science   – page 3
Hodder Gibson Study Skills Advice – General   – page 5
2017 EXAM   – page 7
2018 EXAM   – page 35
2018 SPECIMEN QUESTION PAPER (FOR 2019 EXAM)   – page 63
ANSWERS   – page 97

This book contains the official SQA 2017 and 2018 Exams, and the 2018 Specimen Question Paper for Higher Computing Science, with associated SQA-approved answers modified from the official marking instructions that accompany the paper.

In addition the book contains study skills advice. This advice has been specially commissioned by Hodder Gibson, and has been written by experienced senior teachers and examiners in line with the Higher syllabus and assessment outlines. This is not SQA material but has been devised to provide further guidance for Higher examinations.

Hodder Gibson is grateful to the copyright holders, as credited on the final page of the Answer section, for permission to use their material. Every effort has been made to trace the copyright holders and to obtain their permission for the use of copyright material. Hodder Gibson will be happy to receive information allowing us to rectify any error or omission in future editions.

Hachette UK's policy is to use papers that are natural, renewable and recyclable products and made from wood grown in sustainable forests. The logging and manufacturing processes are expected to conform to the environmental regulations of the country of origin.

Orders: please contact Bookpoint Ltd, 130 Park Drive, Milton Park, Abingdon, Oxon OX14 4SE. Telephone: (44) 01235 827827. Fax: (44) 01235 400454. Lines are open 9.00–5.00, Monday to Saturday, with a 24-hour message answering service. Visit our website at www.hoddereducation.co.uk. Hodder Gibson can also be contacted directly at hoddergibson@hodder.co.uk

This collection first published in 2018 by
Hodder Gibson, an imprint of Hodder Education,
An Hachette UK Company
211 St Vincent Street
Glasgow G2 5QY

Higher 2017 and 2018 Exam Papers and Answers; 2018 Specimen Question Paper and Answers © Scottish Qualifications Authority. Study Skills section © Hodder Gibson. All rights reserved. Apart from any use permitted under UK copyright law, no part of this publication may be reproduced or transmitted in any form or by any means, electronic or mechanical, including photocopying and recording, or held within any information storage and retrieval system, without permission in writing from the publisher or under licence from the Copyright Licensing Agency Limited. Further details of such licences (for reprographic reproduction) may be obtained from the Copyright Licensing Agency Limited, www.cla.co.uk

Typeset by Aptara, Inc.

Printed in the UK

A catalogue record for this title is available from the British Library

ISBN: 978-1-5104-5674-7

2 1

2019 2018

Introduction

Higher Computing Science

This book of SQA past papers contains the question papers used in the 2017 and 2018 exams (with the answers at the back of the book). A specimen question paper reflecting the requirements, content and duration of the revised exam from 2019 is also included. All of the question papers included in the book provide excellent, representative practice for the final exams.

Using the 2017 and 2018 past papers as part of your revision will help you to develop the vital skills and techniques needed for the exam, and will help you to identify any knowledge gaps you may have.

It is always a very good idea to refer to SQA's website for the most up-to-date course specification documents. Further details can be found in the Higher Computing Science section on the SQA website: https://www.sqa.org.uk/sqa/56924.html

The course

Although you may have passed National 5 Computing Science, it is important to understand that the step up to Higher is demanding and may require a different approach to ensure your success. To understand a course at Higher level often requires that you fully understand one fact before you move on to the next. If you leave a lesson confused, do something about it. Read over your notes again in the evening, ask your teacher for further explanation, attend study groups, use the world wide web for research or ask your friends for help. Whichever route you take, make sure that you get into this habit early on in the year.

The exam

The Higher Computing Science course has a question paper which contains two sections and 110 marks (the assignment accounts for 50 marks, giving a total of 160 marks for the course).

Candidates will complete the question paper in 2 hours 30 minutes.

Section 1 contains 25 marks and consists of short-answer questions. Most questions will have 1–2 marks.

Section 2 contains 85 marks and consists of extended-response questions, each with approximately 8–12 marks.

Questions will be of a problem-solving nature rather than direct recall and will include extended descriptions and explanations.

Marks available in the exam paper will be spread across the four areas of the course, as follows:

- approximately 40% for *Software Design and Development*
- approximately 10% for *Computer Systems*
- approximately 25% for *Database Design and Development*
- approximately 25% for *Web Design and Development*

Software Design and Development will include questions from the following areas:

- Development methodologies
- Analysis
- Design
- Implementation, including data types and structures, computational constructs and standard algorithms
- Testing
- Evaluation.

Questions related to programming will use the form of 'pseudocode' below:

Variable types: INTEGER, REAL, BOOLEAN, CHARACTER
Structured types: ARRAY, STRING, RECORD
Subprogram: PROCEDURE, FUNCTION
System entities: DISPLAY, KEYBOARD
Assignment: SET … TO …
Conditions: IF … THEN … (ELSE) … END IF
Conditional repetition: WHILE … DO … END WHILE
REPEAT … UNTIL …
Fixed repetition: REPEAT … TIMES … END REPEAT
Iteration: FOR … FROM … TO … DO … END FOR
FOR EACH … FROM … DO … END FOR EACH
Input/output: RECEIVE … FROM … ,
SEND … TO … , OPEN, CLOSE, CREATE
Operations: -, +, *, /, ^, mod, &
Comparisons: =, ≠, <, <=, >, >=
Logical operators: AND, OR, NOT
Pre-defined functions: id(parameters)

If you are required to write in code then you can use any programming language with which you are familiar or write your answer in pseudocode.

Computer Systems will include questions from the following areas:

- Data representation
- Computer structure
- Environmental impact
- Security risks and precautions.

Database Design and Development will include questions from the following areas:

- Analysis
- Design
- Implementation
- Testing
- Evaluation.

Web Design and Development will include questions from the following areas:
- Analysis
- Design
- Implementation, including CSS, HTML and JavaScript
- Testing
- Evaluation

Question types

The Computing Science exam comprises very few questions that simply ask you to write down or explain a fact or skill you have learned.

The majority of questions involve problem solving – questions where you are required to apply your knowledge to an unfamiliar scenario.

Unseen exam questions will go some way towards preparing you for problem-solving questions but you may find that you quickly run out of new examples. Try making up your own question scenarios and swap them with a friend. Write your own programs, develop a website or create a database of your own, query it and create a variety of reports from the data. You'll find that the task of making up the questions or scenarios in a problem-solving context is a useful exercise in itself.

General advice

Remember to read the questions carefully and answer what is being asked.

Trade names

It is never acceptable to use a company name in an answer such as Microsoft Access, Serif Web-Plus, etc. Use the generic terms such as Databases and Web-Design packages.

Conversion

If you are asked to convert a number into an 8-bit binary number, make sure that your answer has 8 bits!

Technical terminology

It is important that the correct technical terminology is used, e.g. USB Flash Drive – not USB pen, USB stick, Pen Drive or other commonly used expressions.

Data structures

The data structures you are required to know at Higher are parallel one-dimensional arrays, records and sequential files. Remember that arrays are indexed from zero. Practise using arrays of records and accessing data using the correct index and field name.

Memory

Many candidates confuse the RAM memory with Backing Storage. Remember RAM memory is used to store programs and data temporarily while the program is being used. The Backing Storage is used to hold programs and data permanently until you are ready to use them. When you open an application it is taken from the Backing Storage (e.g. Hard Disc Drive) and placed into RAM memory.

Pre-defined functions

Remember that pre-defined functions are built-in sections of code that have been written and tested and are available for programmers to use. They include common functions such as Random Numbers and Rounding.

Parameter passing

An actual parameter is the item of data passed into the subprogram. This will be a value or a variable to be passed in. Actual parameters are named/specified inside the calling program/subprogram. For the time that the called subprogram lasts, the formal parameter – which is named within the called subprogram – will be a pointer to the location of the actual parameter, and any changes made to the formal parameter within the subprogram are automatically made to the actual parameter.

Standard algorithms

Make sure that you have a good understanding and are able to code the standard algorithms required at Higher:
- Find maximum
- Find minimum
- Count occurrences
- Linear search.

Data representation

Among the required knowledge, you will have to know the range of numbers that can be represented using a fixed number of bits using two's complement. The range would be from $-(2^{(x-1)})$ to $(2^{(x-1)})-1$, where x is the number of bits used to store the number.

Intelligent systems

When the question relates to environmental impact of intelligent systems, be sure to comment on features of the system that indicate artificial intelligence – e.g. learning from previous experience.

Implementation

Be sure that you can both write and interpret HTML, CSS, Javascript and SQL at Higher level – ask your teacher for more practice at any that you don't feel confident in.

Good luck!

The most pleasing results for teachers are not necessarily the students who get the "A" pass. It's often the students who achieve their potential, even if that is just scraping a pass. Every year teachers see a few pupils who "could have done better". Don't let that be you!

Remember that the rewards for passing Higher Computing Science are well worth it! Your pass will help you get the future you want for yourself. In the exam, be confident in your own ability. If you're not sure how to answer a question, trust your instincts and give it a go anyway, or move on quickly. Working at a reasonable pace will allow time to return to unanswered questions later. Finally, keep calm and don't panic! GOOD LUCK!

Study Skills – what you need to know to pass exams!

General exam revision: 20 top tips

When preparing for exams, it is easy to feel unsure of where to start or how to revise. This guide to general exam revision provides a good starting place, and, as these are very general tips, they can be applied to all your exams.

1. Start revising in good time.

Don't leave revision until the last minute – this will make you panic and it will be difficult to learn. Make a revision timetable that counts down the weeks to go.

2. Work to a study plan.

Set up sessions of work spread through the weeks ahead. Make sure each session has a focus and a clear purpose. What will you study, when and why? Be realistic about what you can achieve in each session, and don't be afraid to adjust your plans as needed.

3. Make sure you know exactly when your exams are.

Get your exam dates from the SQA website and use the timetable builder tool to create your own exam schedule. You will also get a personalised timetable from your school, but this might not be until close to the exam period.

4. Make sure that you know the topics that make up each course.

Studying is easier if material is in manageable chunks – why not use the SQA topic headings or create your own from your class notes? Ask your teacher for help on this if you are not sure.

5. Break the chunks up into even smaller bits.

The small chunks should be easier to cope with. Remember that they fit together to make larger ideas. Even the process of chunking down will help!

6. Ask yourself these key questions for each course:

- Are all topics compulsory or are there choices?
- Which topics seem to come up time and time again?
- Which topics are your strongest and which are your weakest?

Use your answers to these questions to work out how much time you will need to spend revising each topic.

7. Make sure you know what to expect in the exam.

The subject-specific introduction to this book will help with this. Make sure you can answer these questions:

- How is the paper structured?
- How much time is there for each part of the exam?
- What types of question are involved? These will vary depending on the subject so read the subject-specific section carefully.

8. Past papers are a vital revision tool!

Use past papers to support your revision wherever possible. This book contains the answers and mark schemes too – refer to these carefully when checking your work. Using the mark scheme is useful; even if you don't manage to get all the marks available first time when you first practise, it helps you identify how to extend and develop your answers to get more marks next time – and of course, in the real exam.

9. Use study methods that work well for you.

People study and learn in different ways. Reading and looking at diagrams suits some students. Others prefer to listen and hear material – what about reading out loud or getting a friend or family member to do this for you? You could also record and play back material.

10. There are three tried and tested ways to make material stick in your long-term memory:

- Practising – e.g. rehearsal, repeating
- Organising – e.g. making drawings, lists, diagrams, tables, memory aids
- Elaborating – e.g. incorporating the material into a story or an imagined journey

11. Learn actively.

Most people prefer to learn actively – for example, making notes, highlighting, redrawing and redrafting, making up memory aids, or writing past paper answers. A good way to stay engaged and inspired is to mix and match these methods – find the combination that best suits you. This is likely to vary depending on the topic or subject.

12. Be an expert.
Be sure to have a few areas in which you feel you are an expert. This often works because at least some of them will come up, which can boost confidence.

13. Try some visual methods.
Use symbols, diagrams, charts, flashcards, post-it notes etc. Don't forget – the brain takes in chunked images more easily than loads of text.

14. Remember – practice makes perfect.
Work on difficult areas again and again. Look and read – then test yourself. You cannot do this too much.

15. Try past papers against the clock.
Practise writing answers in a set time. This is a good habit from the start but is especially important when you get closer to exam time.

16. Collaborate with friends.
Test each other and talk about the material – this can really help. Two brains are better than one! It is amazing how talking about a problem can help you solve it.

17. Know your weaknesses.
Ask your teacher for help to identify what you don't know. Try to do this as early as possible. If you are having trouble, it is probably with a difficult topic, so your teacher will already be aware of this – most students will find it tough.

18. Have your materials organised and ready.
Know what is needed for each exam:
- Do you need a calculator or a ruler?
- Should you have pencils as well as pens?
- Will you need water or paper tissues?

19. Make full use of school resources.
Find out what support is on offer:
- Are there study classes available?
- When is the library open?
- When is the best time to ask for extra help?
- Can you borrow textbooks, study guides, past papers, etc.?
- Is school open for Easter revision?

20. Keep fit and healthy!
Try to stick to a routine as much as possible, including with sleep. If you are tired, sluggish or dehydrated, it is difficult to see how concentration is even possible. Combine study with relaxation, drink plenty of water, eat sensibly, and get fresh air and exercise – all these things will help more than you could imagine. Good luck!

HIGHER
2017

H

National Qualifications 2017

FOR OFFICIAL USE

Mark

X716/76/01 **Computing Science**

TUESDAY, 16 MAY
1:00 PM – 3:00 PM

Fill in these boxes and read what is printed below.

Full name of centre

Town

Forename(s)

Surname

Number of seat

Date of birth
Day Month Year

Scottish candidate number

Total marks — 90

SECTION 1 — 20 marks

Attempt ALL questions.

SECTION 2 — 70 marks

Attempt ALL questions.

Show all workings.

Write your answers clearly in the spaces provided in this booklet. Additional space for answers is provided at the end of this booklet. If you use this space you must clearly identify the question number you are attempting.

Use **blue** or **black** ink.

Before leaving the examination room you must give this booklet to the Invigilator; if you do not, you may lose all the marks for this paper.

SECTION 1 — 20 marks
Attempt ALL questions

1. State the range of positive and negative numbers that can be represented using 16 bit two's complement representation. **2**

2. Describe the analysis stage of the software development process. **2**

3. A stereo sound file lasting 2 minutes with a sample rate of 96 kHz and sample depth of 16 bits is stored on a computer.

    Calculate the storage size of the uncompressed sound file.

    Show all working and express your answer in appropriate units. **3**

4. Tables within a database can make use of compound keys and surrogate keys.

   Explain the difference between a compound key and a surrogate key. **2**

5. Tracking cookies can be created and used when browsing a website.

   Describe a security risk associated with tracking cookies. **1**

6. Customers log into their bank account using a username, PIN and password.

   Explain how public and private keys help to keep these details secure when transmitted between the customer and the bank's server. **2**

7. There are many disabilities or impairments that can be a barrier to effective computer use.

(a) Visual impairments could be overcome by using large fonts.

State one other feature that could help a person with a visual impairment. **1**

_____

_____

_____

(b) Hearing impairments could be overcome by adjusting the speaker volume.

State one other feature that could help a person with a hearing impairment. **1**

_____

_____

_____

8. Describe how object-oriented languages are used to create software. **2**

_____

_____

_____

_____

_____

_____

MARKS

9. A programmer is creating a program to store details about books. The details stored are: title, author, number of pages and price.

   (a) Create, using pseudocode or a language with which you are familiar, a record structure to store the book details. **2**

   (b) Declare, using pseudocode or a language with which you are familiar, a variable that can store the data for 1000 books. **2**

[END OF SECTION 1]

[Turn over

SECTION 2 — 70 marks

Attempt ALL Questions

10. HiDoe manufactures intelligent heating control systems that allow users to monitor the temperature in different rooms in their house. An app can be downloaded to access information about energy use.

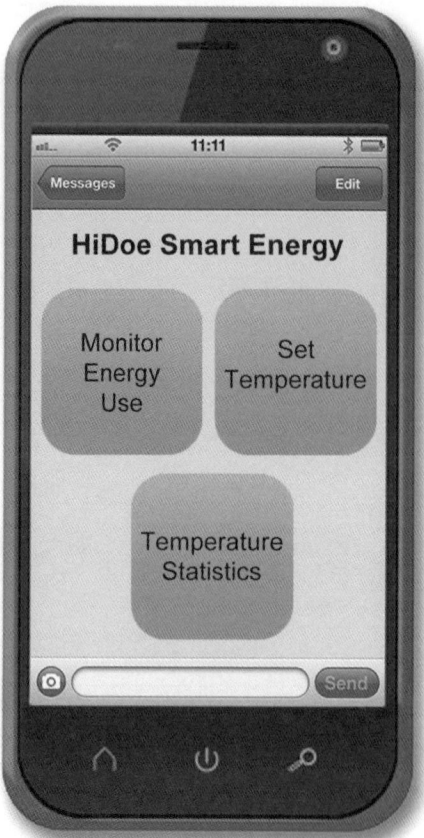

Selecting **Temperature Statistics** on the app allows users to see the highest and lowest temperature of a room over the course of a 24 hour period.

A sensor measures the temperature in a room at the start of each hour in a day. These temperatures are stored in an array called `temps`.

index	0	1	2	3	....	22	23
temps	10	8	12	11	....	14	13

10. **(continued)**

    (a) The temperature statistics feature displays the message:

    The lowest temperature was 8 Celsius at hour 1.

    Write, using pseudocode or a language with which you are familiar, an algorithm that can:
    - find the lowest temperature
    - display the message shown above
    - write the lowest temperature to an external file called "low.txt".

    (b) Name a function of the operating system and describe one task it will perform when creating the external file.

10. (continued)

The app makes use of a function to calculate the average.

Line 1 FUNCTION calcAverage (ARRAY OF INTEGER list) RETURNS INTEGER
Line 2   DECLARE total AS INTEGER INITIALLY 0
Line 3   DECLARE average AS INTEGER INITIALLY 0
Line 4   FOR index FROM 0 TO 23 DO
Line 5   SET total TO total + list[index]
Line 6   SET average TO total / (index +1)
Line 7   END FOR
Line 8   RETURN average
Line 9 END FUNCTION

(c) At the end of the first iteration, the values for total and average are both 10.

   (i) Complete the following trace table to show the values of the total and average variables at the end of the *second and third iteration* of the loop.

End of Iteration	Total	Average
1	10	10
2		
3		

   (ii) On the fourth iteration, a runtime error occurs. Error reporting states that line 6 is the cause.

   Explain why this line causes the problem and how to correct it.

10. (continued)

(d) The calcAverage function only works for 24 integers.

Describe how the function could be altered to calculate the average for any size of list. **1**

(e) Describe two ways that intelligent heating systems such as HiDoe can be used to reduce the carbon footprint of homes. **2**

[Turn over

11. Super Taxi allows users to book taxis from their smartphones. Super Taxi uses a relational database to keep a record of their cars, drivers, bookings and customers.

    Each driver can only drive one car but the same car can be used by more than one driver. The cost is set at the time of booking.

Car	Driver	Booking	Customer
Registration	Driver ID	Booking ID	Customer ID
Make	First Name	From	Known As
Model	Surname	To	Card Number
Licence Expires	Mobile	Cost	Expiry Date
	Registration*	Driver ID*	Authorisation Code
		Customer ID*	

    (a) Draw an entity relationship diagram to show the relationships between the four tables. **3**

11. (continued)

(b) A query is used to generate the report shown below. This report is displayed on a customer's smartphone once a booking is confirmed.

(i) State the tables and fields needed to generate the above report. **3**

(ii) State the search criteria that would identify this booking. **1**

11. (continued)

The following is an extract from the source code used to generate Super Taxi's homepage.

```html
<!DOCTYPE html>
<html>
    <head>
        <title>Super Taxi</title>
    </head>

    <body>

        <h1 id="welcome" onmouseover="mouseOver()"
        onmouseout="mouseOut()">Welcome to Super Taxi</h1>

        <script>
            function mouseOver() {
                document.getElementById("welcome").style.color = "yellow";
            }
            function mouseOut() {
                document.getElementById("welcome").style.color = "black";
            }
        </script>

    </body>
</html>
```

(c) Explain, making reference to the code shown above, what happens when a user places the mouse pointer over the heading "Welcome to Super Taxi". **2**

(d) Meta tags can be used in this webpage.

Insert the missing components of the following meta tag:

<meta _____="keywords" _____="super, taxi"> **2**

11. (continued)

(e) Search engine providers realised that web developers were placing large numbers of keywords in meta tags to improve a website's ranking in search results. This means that meta tags are often ignored by search engines.

Describe two techniques that search engines use to ensure more relevant results are returned. **2**

(f) The following line of code is added to the homepage:

<link rel="stylesheet" type= "text/css" href= "superstyle.css">

State the section of the code in which this line should be placed. **1**

(g) Describe the effect on efficiency of web page load times when comparing external and internal CSS. **2**

12. A program is used to calculate parking charges for a public car park.

The arrival and departure times are converted to and stored as real numbers, for example: 06:30 hours will be converted to and stored as 6.5.

Welcome to Shore Car Park

CHARGES — all charges include VAT

UP TO 1 HOUR   £2·75

UP TO 2 HOURS   £4·25

OVER 2 HOURS   £6·25

The function below is used to calculate the cost of parking for each car.

```
Line 1      FUNCTION calcCost(REAL departure, REAL arrival) RETURNS REAL
Line 1         DECLARE hours_parked INITIALLY 0
Line 3         DECLARE parking_charge INITIALLY 0
Line 4         SET hours_parked TO departure – arrival
Line 5         IF hours_parked <= 1 THEN
Line 6            SET parking_charge TO 2.75
Line 7         ELSE
Line 8            IF hours_parked <=2 THEN
Line 9               SET parking_charge TO 4.25
Line 10           ELSE
Line 11              SET parking_charge TO 6.25
Line 12           END IF
Line 13        END IF
Line 14        RETURN parking_charge
Line 15     END FUNCTION
```

This function is called using the line below:

SET cost TO calcCost (arrived, left)

(a) Identify a formal parameter used in the code above and explain what is meant by a formal parameter.   **2**

12. (continued)

(b) A car arrived at the car park at 10:00 and left at 13:00.

When the function is called, arrived has the value 10.0 and left has the value 13.0. The function returns an incorrect cost of 2.75.

Explain why this function did not return the expected value. **2**

(c) Watchpoints are often used during testing.

Describe how watchpoints are used to help programmers locate errors. **2**

(d) The function makes use of a local variable.

Describe two benefits of using local variables. **2**

13. PCBits is an online shopping site which sells computer hardware and software. The diagram below shows a proposed version of their new website.

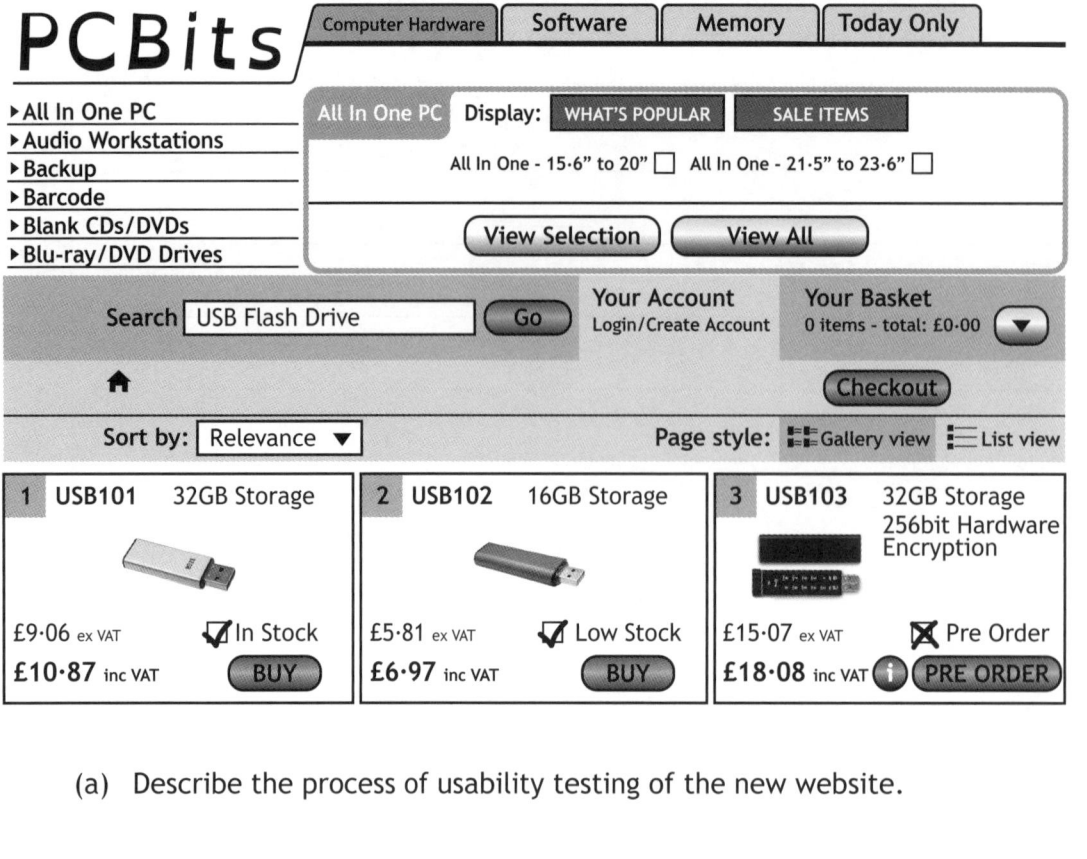

(a) Describe the process of usability testing of the new website. **2**

(b) The website uses both client-side scripting and server-side scripting. Identify one part of the above website generated using client-side scripting. **1**

13. (continued)

(c) Explain how the use of a database driven website would allow the PCBits website to display a message stating whether items are In Stock, Low Stock or available for Pre-Order.

| £9·06 ex VAT ✓ In Stock | £5·81 ex VAT ✓ Low Stock | £15·07 ex VAT ✗ Pre Order |
| £10·87 inc VAT ⓘ BUY | £6·97 inc VAT ⓘ BUY | £18·08 inc VAT ⓘ PRE ORDER |

(d) PCBits is concerned about a loss of data such as customer details and orders.

   (i) Describe a suitable backup schedule for PCBits. Your answer should include a description of the type of backup.

   (ii) Describe one other strategy that could be used to protect against a loss of data.

13. (continued)

(e) The code for one of the webpages is shown below:

```
<!DOCTYPE html>
<html>
    <head>
        <style>
            p{color:red; text-align: center}
        </style>
    </head>

    <body>
        <p> Welcome To </p>
        <p style="color:blue; font-size:200%;"> PCBits</p>
        <p> Glasgow </p>
    </body>
</html>
```

Describe the output from this code. You may use a labelled diagram to support your answer.

2

14. Catherine runs CraftyBella, an online business promoting arts and crafts.

    (a) Catherine is concerned that the business data stored on the public cloud is not secure.

    Explain why this is **not** the case. **2**

    (b) Catherine has designed a black and white logo. There is both a bitmapped and vector graphic of the logo shown below.

    (i) Catherine wants to move the ears of the cat closer together. State whether this task is easier to do with the bitmapped or the vector graphic. Explain your answer. **2**

14. (b) (continued)

(ii) Describe the effect on the file size of adding the star to both the vector **and** bitmapped graphic. 2

15. A manufacturer of mobile phones is considering the SnapLizard processor. A description of the SnapLizard is given below.

> The SnapLizard processor has a clock speed of 2·4 GHz. It is quad core, resulting in extremely efficient multi-tasking when compared to dual core processors. The data bus and the address bus are both 32 bits. The SnapLizard includes a separate instruction and data cache.

(a) The processor runs the machine code version of an application by fetching and executing instructions from memory. Describe the steps of the fetch-execute cycle.   **3**

(b) The SnapLizard includes cache for instructions and data.

   (i) Explain how cache improves performance.   **2**

[Turn over

15. (b) (continued)

(ii) The SnapLizard has many registers including X and Y registers. Here are three low level language instructions that are fetched and executed in sequence:

1	LOAD X, 2000	Loads the contents of memory location with address 2000 into the X register.
2	LOAD Y, 2000	Loads the contents of memory location with address 2000 into the Y register.
3	ADD X, Y	Add the contents of the Y register to the X register.

Explain the impact of cache on the execution of instructions 2 and 3.

2

(c) The mobile phone should be capable of capturing high quality video.

One characteristic that would be considered would be bit depth. Describe the difference between a bit depth of 16 bits and that of 24 bits for the quality of video.

2

15. (continued)

(d) (i) Describe how video is compressed using interframe and intraframe compression. **2**

(ii) The effectiveness of video compression can depend on the content that is being captured. For example, videoing someone sitting singing a song on stage will compress differently when compared to videoing a high energy dance performance with a group of dancers.

Explain the effectiveness of interframe compression for these different performances. **2**

[END OF QUESTION PAPER]

ADDITIONAL SPACE FOR ANSWERS

ADDITIONAL SPACE FOR ANSWERS

[BLANK PAGE]

DO NOT WRITE ON THIS PAGE

HIGHER
2018

FOR OFFICIAL USE

H

National Qualifications 2018

Mark

X716/76/01

Computing Science

TUESDAY, 22 MAY
1:00 PM – 3:00 PM

Fill in these boxes and read what is printed below.

Full name of centre

Town

Forename(s)

Surname

Number of seat

Date of birth
Day Month Year

Scottish candidate number

Total marks — 90

SECTION 1 — 20 marks

Attempt ALL questions.

SECTION 2 — 70 marks

Attempt ALL questions.

Show all workings.

Write your answers clearly in the spaces provided in this booklet. Additional space for answers is provided at the end of this booklet. If you use this space you must clearly identify the question number you are attempting.

Use **blue** or **black** ink.

Before leaving the examination room you must give this booklet to the Invigilator; if you do not, you may lose all the marks for this paper.

SQA

SECTION 1 — 20 marks
Attempt ALL questions

1. Convert the number −120 into 8 bit two's complement. **1**

2. Explain the difference between a public key and a private key when securing the transmission of data. **2**

3. Facts are a feature of a declarative language. An example is shown below:

   `sibling(fred, senga).`

   Name and describe one other feature of a declarative language. **2**

4. Disk mirroring (RAID) is a backup strategy used to create a second copy of data in real time.

   Describe two drawbacks of using mirroring (RAID) as a backup strategy. **2**

5. Character sets can be represented using either ASCII or Unicode.

   Describe an advantage of using Unicode over ASCII, making reference to the number of bits used to represent a character in each format. **2**

6. A database designer may have to make use of a surrogate key.

   Explain what is meant by the term surrogate key. **2**

[Turn over

7. The incomplete function shown below performs a linear search to find the position of the target item in the following array of strings.

| Meena | Sean | Gianni | Ali | Nyah | Lynn |

When Meena is entered as the target item then 0 is returned. If Lynn is entered as the target item then 5 is returned.

```
Line 1   FUNCTION linearSearch(ARRAY OF STRING list)RETURNS
         INTEGER
Line 2      DECLARE index INITIALLY -1
Line 3      DECLARE position INITIALLY -1
Line 4      DECLARE target AS STRING INITIALLY FROM KEYBOARD
Line 5      REPEAT
Line 6         SET index TO index+1
Line 7         IF target=list[index] THEN
Line 8            SET _____
Line 9         END IF
Line 10     UNTIL <end of list> OR _____
Line 11     RETURN position
Line 12  END FUNCTION
```

(a) Complete lines 8 and 10 below.

Line 8 SET _____

Line 10 UNTIL <end of list> OR _____

(b) State the value that would be returned by the function if the target item was not in the list.

8. Machine code instructions are fetched from memory and executed by the processor.

Complete the missing steps of the fetch-execute cycle in the table below. **2**

1.	The processor places the address of the instruction on the address bus.
2.	
3.	
4.	Instruction is decoded and executed.

9. The increased use of cache memory is one trend that improves the performance of modern computer architecture.

(a) State one other trend that improves performance. **1**

(b) Describe how your answer to part (a) improves performance. **1**

[Turn over

10. John has downloaded a new computer game but finds that it does not run on his computer.

(a) State one software reason why the game may not be compatible. **1**

_____

(b) State one hardware reason why the game may not be compatible. **1**

_____

[END OF SECTION 1]

SECTION 2 — 70 marks

Attempt ALL questions

11. SecureBell is a company that manufactures an Internet enabled doorbell which can be accessed using a smartphone. The doorbell has a video camera, which allows the customer to see, hear and speak with anyone arriving at their front door.

    (a) SecureBell stores customer videos on a public cloud.

    (i) State two reasons why SecureBell chooses to use a public cloud rather than a private cloud to store the videos. **2**

    (ii) Customers may have concerns about the security of video being stored on the public cloud.

    State two precautions used to ensure security of data on public cloud storage. **2**

11. (continued)

(b) State two implications of the Regulation of Investigatory Powers Act (RIPA) for SecureBell.

(c) When the doorbell is pressed, the camera captures video with a resolution of 1920 pixels by 1080 pixels, 65 536 colours and a frame rate of 24 frames per second.

(i) Calculate the size of the first frame captured. Express your answer in bits.

(ii) This first frame is compressed using intraframe compression.

Describe how interframe compression is also used to reduce the file size of the video.

11. (continued)

(d) SecureBell is considering changes to their logo and have edited it as shown below.

Original logo   Edited logo

(i) State whether the logo was created in a vector or a bitmap package. Explain your answer. **2**

(ii) Explain how Run Length Encoding would compress this image. **2**

[Turn over

12. A new app is being developed for movie fans.

(a) The developers of the app are using agile methodologies. They employ usability testing as part of this.

Describe how usability testing influences the development of the app. **3**

(b) The app will have information on the top 100 movies of all time including the studio that made the movie, fan ratings and takings at the box office. For example:

Title	Studio	Rating (out of 100)	Takings ($m)
The Matrice	Nightworks	85	6.7
The Home Route	Gateway	42	0.4
Freezing	Aurora	95	12.5
....	.....	......	......

(i) Using pseudocode or a programming language of your choice, define a suitable record data structure for the movie data above. **2**

12. (b) (continued)

(ii) Using pseudocode or a programming language of your choice, declare the variable which can store the details of the top 100 movies.

Your answer should use the record data structure created in part (i). **2**

(c) Using pseudocode or a programming language of your choice, write an algorithm which:

- asks for a studio name
- totals the number of movies that the studio has in the top 100
- saves the studio name and total to file. **6**

Page eleven [Turn over

13. A tourist website has a web page which displays statistics about towns and cities. The user enters a name in the text box and clicks on the search button to display the statistics.

(a) Explain why server-side scripting has been used to produce the statistics as shown on the web page above. **1**

(b) The website makes use of Cascading Style Sheets (CSS)

(i) The text 'Glasgow Statistics' is an H1 heading. Write a CSS rule that makes H1 headings appear in Arial, centre aligned and green. **3**

(ii) Describe how CSS rules should be implemented to ensure that all of the web pages on the website have consistent formatting. **2**

13. (continued)

(c) When the user places their mouse on the image of Glasgow's coat of arms it increases in size as shown below. When the mouse is moved away from the image, the image returns to its normal size.

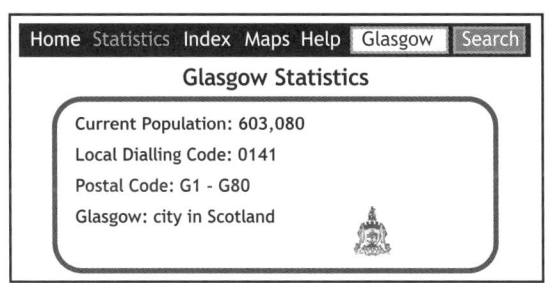

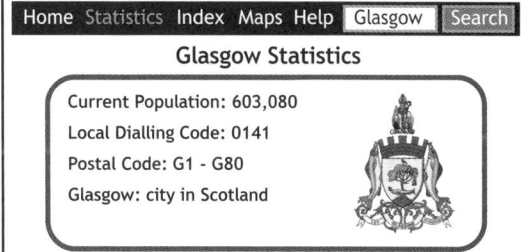

Complete the four missing lines of code to allow the:

- Function Increase() to triple the width and height of the graphic when the user moves the mouse pointer over the image
- Function Normal() to return the image to its original size when the user moves the mouse pointer off the image.

3

```
<!DOCTYPE html>
<html>
<body>

<img
onmouseover="Increase(this)"
onmouseout="_____"
src="Glasgow.png"
width="32" height="32">

<script>
function Increase(x) {
    x.style.width = "96px";
    _____
}

function Normal(x) {
    _____

    _____
}
</script>

</body>
</html>
```

Page thirteen [Turn over

13. (continued)

(d) The user tries to find statistics for Aberdeen. However, they typed "Aberdene" into the text box and the following web page was displayed.

> Home Statistics Index Maps Help | Aberdene | Search
>
> **Aberdene Statistics**
>
> Results of Search for "Aberdene"
>
> Sorry, we found no match for your location

Explain how this database-driven website uses server-side scripting to produce the output above.

4

[Turn over for next question

DO NOT WRITE ON THIS PAGE

14. GlenSki offers one-to-one skiing lessons at a number of ski resorts in Scotland.

Instructors are based at a resort, and customers can book several lessons on one day.

A relational database is used to store data as follows:

Customer	Lesson	Resort	Instructor
CustomerID	InstructorID*	ResortID	InstructorID
FirstName	StartTime	Name	FirstName
Surname	Date	Postcode	Surname
ContactNumber	Duration	Lifts	ResortID*
EmailAddress	CustomerID*		

(a) Draw an entity relationship diagram to show the relationships that exist in this database.

3

14. (continued)

(b) State the primary key used to uniquely identify the Lesson table. **1**

_____

_____

(c) The following report was generated to show an instructor a list of the lessons that they will deliver on a specific date.

> GlenSki   17/12/18   Instructor: 14
>
> Daily Schedule   Chris, your lessons today are:
>
> Rafal Avila   9.00 am
> Martin Iskra   11.00 am
> Daniella Smith   12.15 pm
> Rafal Avila   3.00 pm
>
> Number of lessons: 4

State the tables and fields needed to output the above report. **3**

14. (continued)

(d) The report was based on the result of a query.

State the criteria used to select the data shown in the report. **2**

(e) State the report feature that has been used to display the 'Number of lessons' shown as part of this report. **1**

(f) GlenSki wants to expand their business worldwide.

Describe one potential business cost of scaling their information systems. **1**

(g) GlenSki encourages customers to participate in an online community.

Describe one benefit to customers of joining an online community. **1**

[Turn over for next question

DO NOT WRITE ON THIS PAGE

15. SportsStats is a program that processes the results of athletics competitions. The results of two different heats are compared to find which heat had the fastest time.

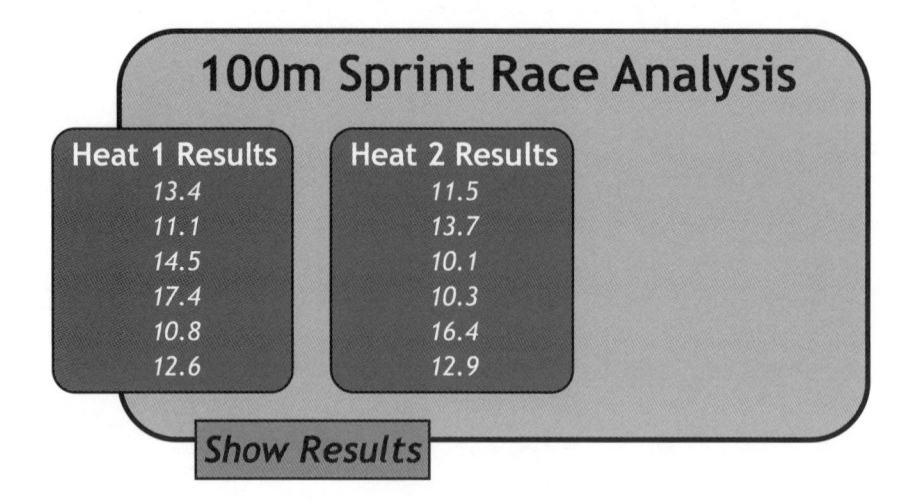

100m Sprint Race Analysis

Heat 1 Results	Heat 2 Results
13.4	11.5
11.1	13.7
14.5	10.1
17.4	10.3
10.8	16.4
12.6	12.9

Show Results

When a user presses the 'Show Results' button, the program should output the number of the heat that had the fastest runner, for example:

"The fastest runner ran in heat 2"

The program makes use of the following function:

```
Line 1    FUNCTION fastest_time(ARRAY OF REAL list) RETURNS REAL
Line 2       DECLARE min INITIALLY list[0]
Line 3       DECLARE upper INITIALLY length(list[])
Line 4       FOR index FROM 1 to (upper-1) DO
Line 5          IF min < list[index] THEN
Line 6             SET min TO list[index]
Line 7          END IF
Line 8       END FOR
Line 9       RETURN min
Line 10   END FUNCTION
```

The function is used in the following section of code:
...
```
Line 21   SET heat1 TO [13.4, 11.1, 14.5, 17.4, 10.8, 12.6]
Line 22   SET heat2 TO [11.5, 13.7, 10.1, 10.3, 16.4, 12.9]
Line 23   SET first_result TO fastest_time (heat1)
Line 24   SET second_result TO fastest_time (heat2)
Line 25   IF first_result < second_result THEN
Line 26      SEND "The fastest runner ran in heat 1" TO DISPLAY
Line 27   ELSE
Line 28      SEND "The fastest runner ran in heat 2" TO DISPLAY
Line 29   END IF
```
...

15. (continued)

(a) Explain why line 4 of the function contains the limit (upper-1). **1**

_____

_____

(b) Describe how the parameters are used when executing line 23.
Your answer should identify the formal and actual parameters. **3**

_____

_____

_____

_____

_____

_____

(c) State the scope of the min variable. Explain your answer. **2**

_____

_____

_____

(d) Testing reveals an error in the function. The function is first called during execution of line 23 of the main program.

In order to identify this error, a watchpoint has been set to show the value of the min variable each time it is changed.

Complete the table to show the values that would be shown when this watchpoint is triggered. **3**

Function Line	min
2	
6	
6	

15. (continued)

(e) Testers report that the program sometimes outputs the incorrect result.

(i) Identify the error in the function that causes incorrect output. **1**

(ii) State the type of error that has caused this issue. **1**

(iii) Explain why the incorrect code outputs the correct statement.

Your answer should make reference to the original heat results shown on lines 21 and 22 of the code. **2**

15. (continued)

(f) If the fastest time in heat 1 and heat 2 is the same, the following output is always displayed:

"The fastest runner ran in heat 2"

(i) Explain this output with reference to the conditional statement beginning at line 25.   **2**

(ii) Explain how the code could be altered to include a third option which will state:

"Both heats have the identical fastest time"   **1**

(g) Explain the role of the memory management function of the operating system when a user loads the SportsStats program.   **2**

[END OF QUESTION PAPER]

ADDITIONAL SPACE FOR ANSWERS

ADDITIONAL SPACE FOR ANSWERS

HIGHER
2018 Specimen Question Paper

H

National Qualifications
SPECIMEN ONLY

FOR OFFICIAL USE

Mark

S816/76/01   **Computing Science**

Date — Not applicable
Duration — 2 hours 30 minutes

Fill in these boxes and read what is printed below.

Full name of centre

Town

Forename(s)

Surname

Number of seat

Date of birth
Day   Month   Year

Scottish candidate number

Total marks — 110

SECTION 1 — 25 marks

Attempt ALL questions.

SECTION 2 — 85 marks

Attempt ALL questions.

Show all workings.

Write your answers clearly in the spaces provided in this booklet. Additional space for answers is provided at the end of this booklet. If you use this space you must clearly identify the question number you are attempting.

Use **blue** or **black** ink.

Before leaving the examination room you must give this booklet to the Invigilator; if you do not, you may lose all the marks for this paper.

SQA

SECTION 1 — 25 marks
Attempt ALL questions

1. Convert the following 16-bit two's complement number into denary.

   1111 1110 1110 1011

2. A developer and their client are based in different time zones in the world.

   Explain the impact that this can have when using an agile methodology compared to an iterative one.

3. A website is subject to a DOS attack.

   State two symptoms users experience when this happens.

4. A database table is shown below.

Table: Model

category	partID	partName	stockQuantity	price
A	23	25cm straight track	7	5.99
B	56	passenger	9	2.99
B	34	luggage	42	2.79
A	98	15cm curve track	15	6.99
B	69	dog	6	0.50
A	29	15cm straight track	20	3.50
A	64	t-shaped junction	18	2.00

Complete the table below showing the output from the following SQL statement.

```
SELECT category, MAX(price) AS [Most expensive item]
FROM Model
GROUP BY category;
```

category	Most expensive item

5. Describe one problem that can occur when using global variables in a program.

[Turn over

6. A text file stores the names of players and the time (in seconds) that they took to complete a game. Players who played the game more than once appear more than once in the file, as shown below.

   ...
   Harry,1745
   Gemma,1028
   Jeremy,1209
   Harry,1358
   ...

   The following algorithm is used to access data in the file.

   1. Enter target player's name
   2. Open file
   3. Start conditional loop
   4.   Read name and time from file
   5.   If name is equal to target player's name then
   6.   store time as fastest time
   7.   End if
   8. Repeat until first instance of target player's name is found in the data file
   9. Start conditional loop from current position in file
   10.   Read name and time from file
   11.   If name is equal to target player's name then
   12.   If time is less than stored fastest time
   13.   store new fastest time
   14.   End if
   15.   End if
   16. Repeat until end of file
   17. Display target player's name and fastest time
   18. Close file

   (a) Describe the purpose of the following steps in the algorithm.

   (i) Steps 3 to 8 _____ 1

   _____

   (ii) Steps 9 to 16 _____ 1

   _____

   (b) A program is written using the above algorithm. A user enters a name in step 1 that is not present in the text file.

   State the execution error that would occur. 1

   _____

   _____

7. The following HTML code and JavaScript functions change the size of a graphic as the mouse arrow passes over and out of the graphic.

```
<img src="guitar.jpg" onmouseover="displayLarger(this)"
onmouseout="displaySmaller(this)">
<script>
    function displayLarger(my_image)
    {my_image.style.width='150px';
    my_image.style.height='150px';}
    function displaySmaller(my_image)
    {my_image.style.width='100px';
    my_image.style.height='100px';}
</script>
```

Write HTML code with a JavaScript function that would permanently display the graphic at 300 × 300 pixels when the graphic is clicked.

3

8. Many sports clubs in Scotland have one president but they have many members. A member can only belong to one club.

Complete the entity-occurrence diagram below to represent the relationship between clubs, presidents and members.

2

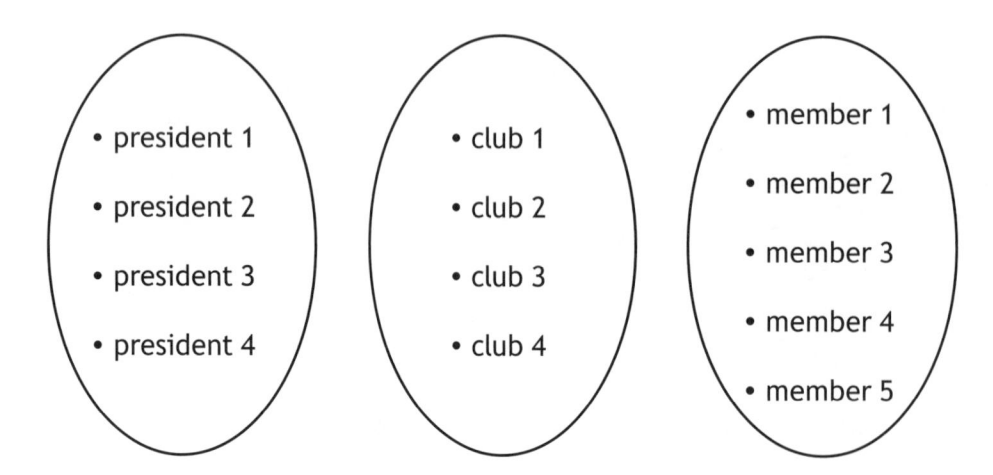

- president 1
- president 2
- president 3
- president 4

- club 1
- club 2
- club 3
- club 4

- member 1
- member 2
- member 3
- member 4
- member 5

9. Convert 0·001011 to floating-point representation. There are 16 bits for the mantissa and 8 bits for the exponent.

3

Space for working

sign | mantissa | exponent

10. Wireframe designs of web pages show the position and characteristics of media to be used.

State one other element that could be shown on a wireframe design. **1**

11. Two computer systems have the same number of processor cores, the same width of data bus and the same clock speed.

(a) State one other factor that could account for one computer system performing better than the other, when tested for processing speed. **1**

(b) Explain why increasing the width of the data bus will improve the system performance. **2**

12. Describe the role of public and private keys when transferring secure data. **2**

13. Describe how a walkthrough of a low-fidelity prototype of a website can identify problems with the navigation design. **1**

SECTION 2 — 85 marks
Attempt ALL questions

14. The International Bowling Federation maintains a relational database that consists of three linked tables, storing data on players, tournaments and tournament entries.

    Extracts from these tables are shown below.

    Tournament

tournamentID	country	place	eventDate
1	UK	Preston	13/05/2017
2	France	Le Mans	29/08/2017
3	USA	Miami	08/09/2017
4	Germany	Berlin	12/03/2018
...	...	...	...

    Player

playerID	forename	surname	rating	playerCountry
1645	Barry	Simpson	1756	USA
1873	Sue	Pollock	1260	Australia
2093	Ahmed	Ali	1934	UK
...	...	...	...	...

    Entry

tournamentID	position	prizeMoney	playerID
1	1	15000	1645
1	2	7000	1873
1	3	1000	9834
2	1	12000	1873
2	2	6000	1842
2	3	1500	9023
3	1	30000	1873
3	2	22000	1009
3	3	15000	0293
3	4	5000	3742
...	...	...	...

Page eight

14. (continued)

    (a) Identify the compound key used in the Federation's database. **2**

    (b) Sue Pollock asks for a list of all the prize money she has won, along with the position she finished in when she won each prize.

    The Federation implements the design shown below:

    Query 1 — All Entries for Sue Pollock

Field(s) and calculation(s)	position, prizeMoney
Table(s) and query	Player, Result
Search criteria	forename = "Sue", surname = "Pollock"
Grouping	
Sort order	

    The answer table from Query 1 could then be used in Query 2 to find the largest amount of money Sue Pollock won when she finished first in a tournament (position 1).

    Complete the design for Query 2 to find this value. **3**

    Query 2 — Display largest amount of money when finishing first

Field(s) and calculation(s)	
Table(s) and query	
Search criteria	
Grouping	
Sort order	

[Turn over

14. (continued)

(c) The Federation writes the following SQL statement to find how many times each country has awarded prizes of over 7000.

```
SELECT country, COUNT(prizeMoney)
FROM Tournament, Entry
WHERE prizeMoney > 7000
AND Tournament.tournamentID = Player.tournamentID
GROUP BY country;
```

(i) State the purpose of the GROUP BY line of the SQL statement. **1**

(ii) The expected output of the SQL statement is shown below.

Country	Over 7000
USA	17
Canada	5
Australia	6
UK	12

When the SQL statement was tested, the actual output did not match the expected output.

Identify two errors in the SQL statement. **2**

Error 1 _____

Error 2 _____

14. (continued)

(d) The Federation retains 10% of the total prize money.

Write the SQL statement that would produce the following output. **3**

Retained prize money
1700000

(e) Each player can only be a member of one bowling club.

Complete the entity-relationship diagram below to show how the club could be added to the database. **2**

Tournament —has—< Entry >—made by— Player

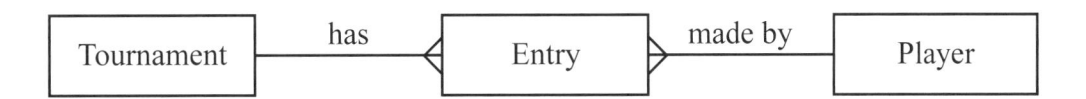

Club

[Turn over

15. An estate agent is developing a website. A horizontal navigation bar will include links to two departments: residential property and commercial property. Customers should be able to read department pages for either renting or buying.

(a) Design a multi-level structure for the estate agent's website. **2**

15. (continued)

(b) A wireframe design for the residential property page is shown below.

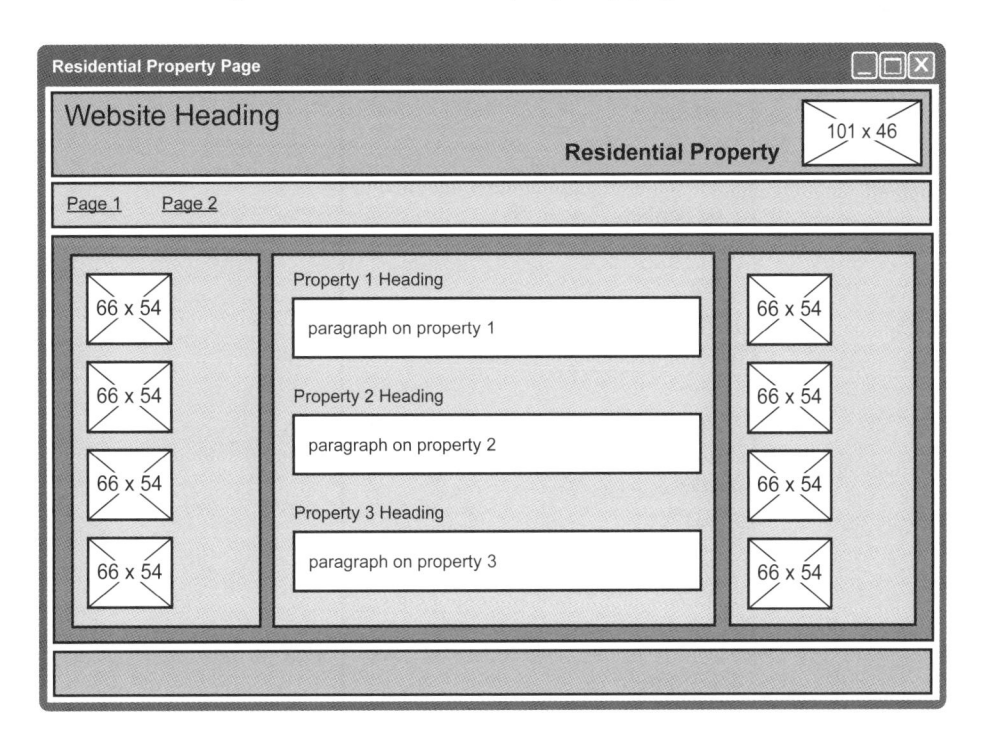

When the page is implemented, the margins and padding are coded as follows:

```
header {margin-top:5px; margin-bottom:5px; padding:10px}
nav {margin-top:5px; margin-bottom:5px; padding:10px}
main {margin-top:5px; margin-bottom:5px; padding:10px}
footer {margin-top:5px; padding:5px}
section {margin-left:10px; margin-top:10px; padding:5px}
```

Using grouping selectors to remove any repetition, re-write the code to make it more efficient.

4

15. (continued)

(c) Property sellers can register with the estate agent using a form on the website.

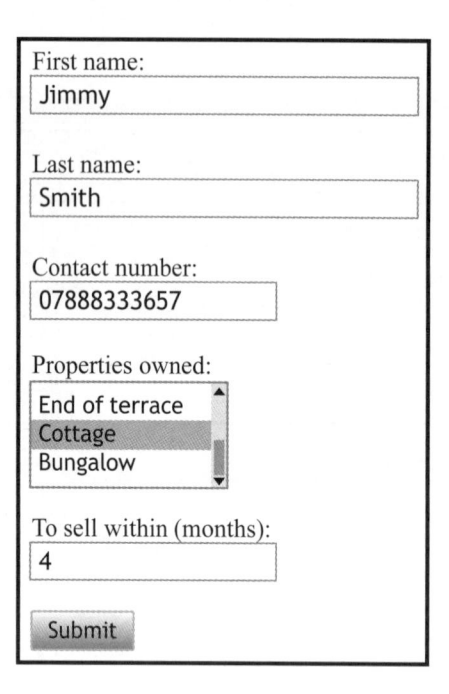

The HTML code for the form is shown below.

```
<form>
First name:<br>
<input type="text" name="firstname" size="30" maxlength="15" required> <br><br>
Last name:<br>
<input type="text" name="lastname" size="30" maxlength="15" required> <br><br>
Contact Number:<br>
<input type="text" name="class" size="20" maxlength="11" required> <br><br>
Properties Owned:<br>
<select name="propertyType" multiple size="3">
    <option value="flat">Flat</option>
    <option value="detached">Detached</option>
    <option value="semiDetached">Semi-detached
    </option>
    <option value="terrace">Terrace</option>
    <option value="endTerrace">End of terrace
    </option>
    <option value="cottage">Cottage</option>
    <option value="bungalow">Bungalow</option>
</select> <br><br>
To Sell Within (months):<br>
<input type="number" name="sale"> <br><br>
<input type="submit" onclick="alert('Form Entered')" value="Submit">
</form>
```

15. (c) (continued)

(i) Identify two types of data validation used in the form code. **2**

Type 1 _____

Type 2 _____

(ii) State the number of property types that a seller can select. **1**

_____

_____

(iii) Cottages always sell quickly, so the estate agent wishes to limit the maximum value that can be entered into 'To sell within (months)' to 3.

To achieve this, they edit the form as shown below.

```
To sell within (months):<br>
<input type="number" name="sale" max="3">
```

Evaluate if this change makes the form fit for purpose. **1**

_____

_____

_____

_____

(d) Before the website goes live, it needs to be tested.

(i) State two compatibility tests that could be carried out. **2**

Test 1 _____

Test 2 _____

(ii) Explain the role of personas and test cases in usability testing. **2**

Personas _____

_____

Test cases _____

_____

[Turn over

16. The Caesar cypher is a simple encryption method that takes each letter in a message and changes it to a different letter.

The program below asks the user to enter a message and an integer used to change the letters in the string.

Both inputs are passed to a function that generates and returns an encrypted version of the message.

```
...
Line 11   FUNCTION encryptString (STRING messageText,
          INTEGER change) RETURNS STRING
Line 12       DECLARE newMessage INITIALLY ""
Line 13       DECLARE characterValue INITIALLY 0
Line 14       DECLARE character INITIALLY ""
Line 15       FOR index FROM 0 TO LEN(messageText)-1
Line 16           SET character TO messagetext[index]
Line 17           SET characterValue TO <ascii value of
                  character> + change
Line 18           SET newMessage TO newMessage & <character
                  equivalent of characterValue>
Line 19       END FOR
Line 20       RETURN newMessage
Line 21   END FUNCTION
...
...
Line 52   RECEIVE message FROM STRING KEYBOARD
Line 53   RECEIVE shiftLettersBy FROM INTEGER KEYBOARD
Line 54   SET message TO
          encryptString(message,shiftLettersBy)
Line 55   DISPLAY message
...
```

(a) The above code contains actual parameters and formal parameters.

Identify an actual parameter in the code. **1**

(b) A breakpoint is set at line 19.

The function is tested by entering the two inputs shown below.

Input 1: cab

Input 2: 3

Complete the table below to show the values of `character` and `newMessage` each time execution is stopped. **3**

Break in execution	Character	newMessage
First		
Second		
Third		

16. (continued)

(c) Using a programming language of your choice, state the pre-defined function used to convert:

    (i) Character to ASCII _____ **1**

    (ii) ASCII to Character _____ **1**

(d) An execution error occurs for some values of `message` or `shiftLettersBy`.

Explain why this happens. **1**

[Turn over

16. (continued)

(e) The function could be re-written to reverse the characters in the message string. For example, inputting 'jfx' would produce the output 'xfj'.

Using a recognised design technique, design an algorithm to reverse and store the new message.

3

17. In Formula One motor racing, teams can enter two drivers for each race. Every driver has a unique number on their car, which is allocated annually at the start of each new racing season.

A database is required to store data on the teams, drivers and race results since the sport started in 1950. Users would be able to collate information on team or driver wins to find the most successful racers or find how the success of teams has changed over the years.

(a) State two functional requirements of the above database. **2**

_____

_____

_____

(b) The entity-relationship diagram below shows how information on the teams, drivers and the races since 1950 could be stored. There are errors in the design.

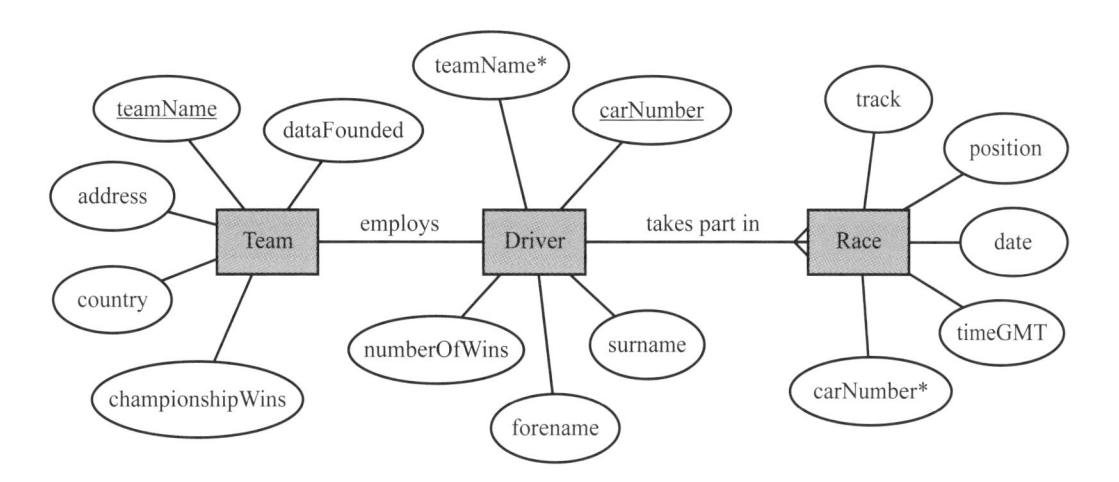

Describe three errors in the above design. **3**

Error 1 _____

_____

Error 2 _____

_____

Error 3 _____

_____

[Turn over

17. (continued)

(c) The Team table is shown below.

Table: Team			
teamName	country	dateFounded	championshipWins
Red Bull	Austria	13/08/2005	4
Ferrari	Italy	01/10/1950	15
Lotus	UK	30/05/1967	6
Force India	India	02/02/2008	0
Benetton	UK	09/10/1986	2
Maserati	Italy	10/01/1950	6
McLaren	UK	07/07/1966	12
Matra	France	30/06/1962	1
Toro Rosso	Italy	12/11/2006	0
Williams	UK	09/11/1978	7
Renault	France	28/03/1977	2
Brawn GP	UK	01/04/2009	1
Mercedes	Germany	29/12/1954	6

(i) Complete the table below to show the output from the following SQL statement.

```
SELECT country, SUM(championshipWins)
FROM Team
GROUP BY country
ORDER BY country ASC;
```

country	championshipWins
Austria	4
	3
Germany	6
India	0
Italy	
UK	28

17. (c) (continued)

(ii) Design a query using wildcards, to find and display all the teams formed in the 1950s.

2

Field(s) and calculation(s)	
Table(s)	Team
Search criteria	
Grouping	
Sort order	

[Turn over

18. The BigIQ Company stores the results for an intelligence test in an external csv file. The data includes each participant's unique ID number, name, town and score.

An extract, is shown below.

0622737819,Jim,Smith,Stirling,73
0872267103,Alison,Jones,Fort William,81
2289448103,Ali,Khan,Dumfries,51

There are 5000 participants listed in the csv file. The BigIQ Company wants to find and display the name of the town for the participant with the highest score.

(a) The data from the file is imported into an array of records.

(i) Using a programming language of your choice, define a suitable record structure. **3**

(ii) Using a programming language of your choice, declare a variable that can store the data for 5000 participants. **2**

18. (continued)

(b) Using a programming language of your choice, write the code to find the position of the highest score.

4

(c) A participant manages to access the file and change their own score.

State two different offences the participant has committed under the Computer Misuse Act 1990.

2

[Turn over

19. Turner High School's English department has designed a website to suggest home reading lists for each year group. Students can access the website on multiple device types.

An annotated wireframe design for one page of the website is shown below.

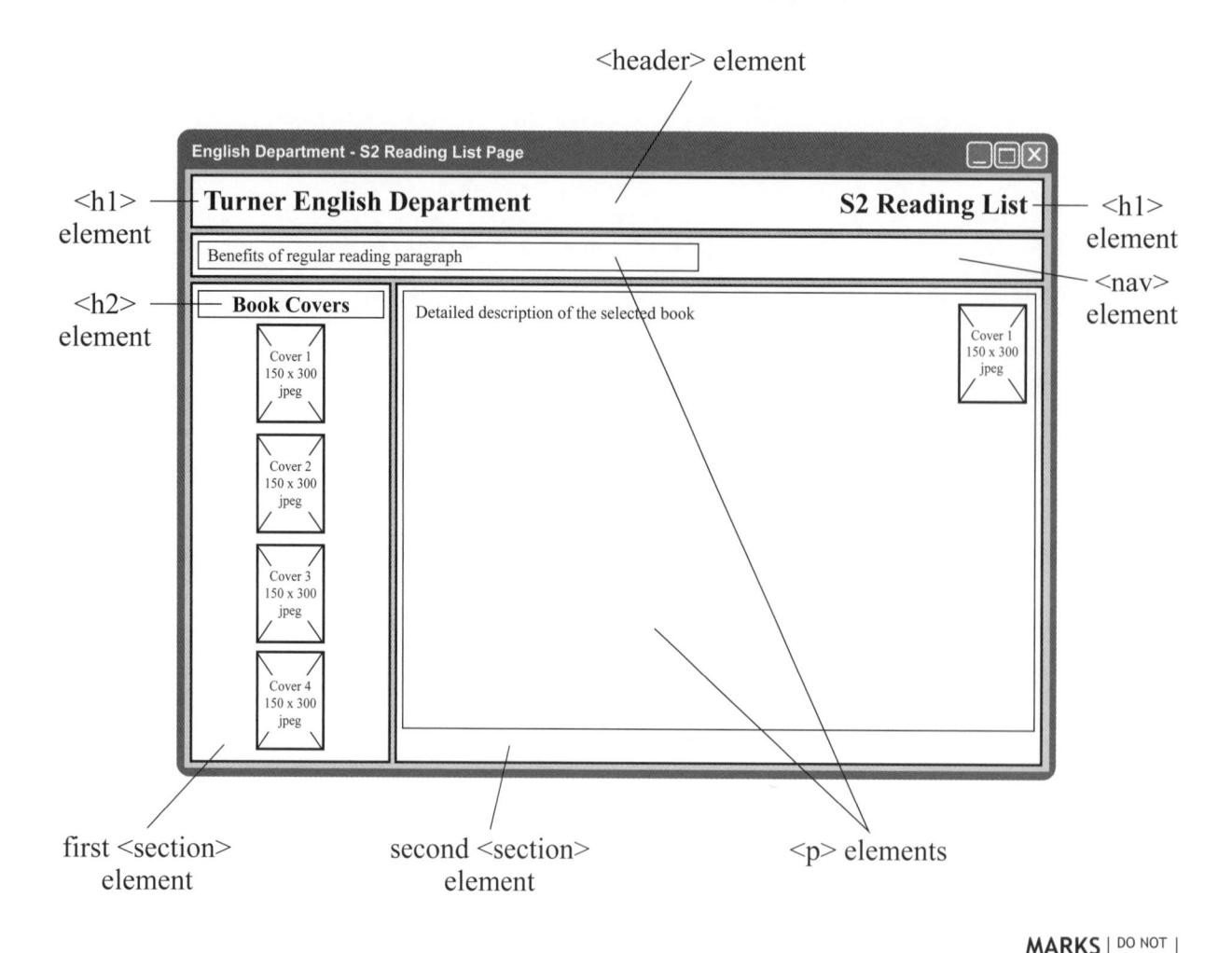

(a) Describe two flaws in the above design that could result in an ineffective user interface.

2

19. (continued)

(b) The detailed description text will wrap around the image by floating the image to the right of the paragraph.

Identify two other layout requirements shown in the wireframe where a CSS float property may be required.

2

Area 1 _____

Area 2 _____

(c) The web page is coded using an external CSS file. Part of the code is shown below.

```
...
body {background-color:LightGreen;margin:auto}
header, nav, section {margin-bottom:5px;background-color:LightGrey}
p {margin-top:5px;background-color:White;display:inline}
h1, h2, h3, p {font-family:Helvetica;color:Black}
section p {color:DarkGreen;padding:10px}
...
```

The book descriptions are tested by displaying the page in a browser.

Describe the expected results for the book descriptions, using the code and the annotations on the wireframe.

You should describe both the expected look and relative positions of the text.

4

[Turn over

19. (continued)

(d) When visiting the web page, users can click on a book cover to see a description of the book. The description, along with a copy of the book cover, will then appear in the main area of the page.

English Department - S2 Reading List Page

Turner English Department — **S2 Reading List**

Benefits of regular reading paragraph

Book Covers — Detailed description of the selected book

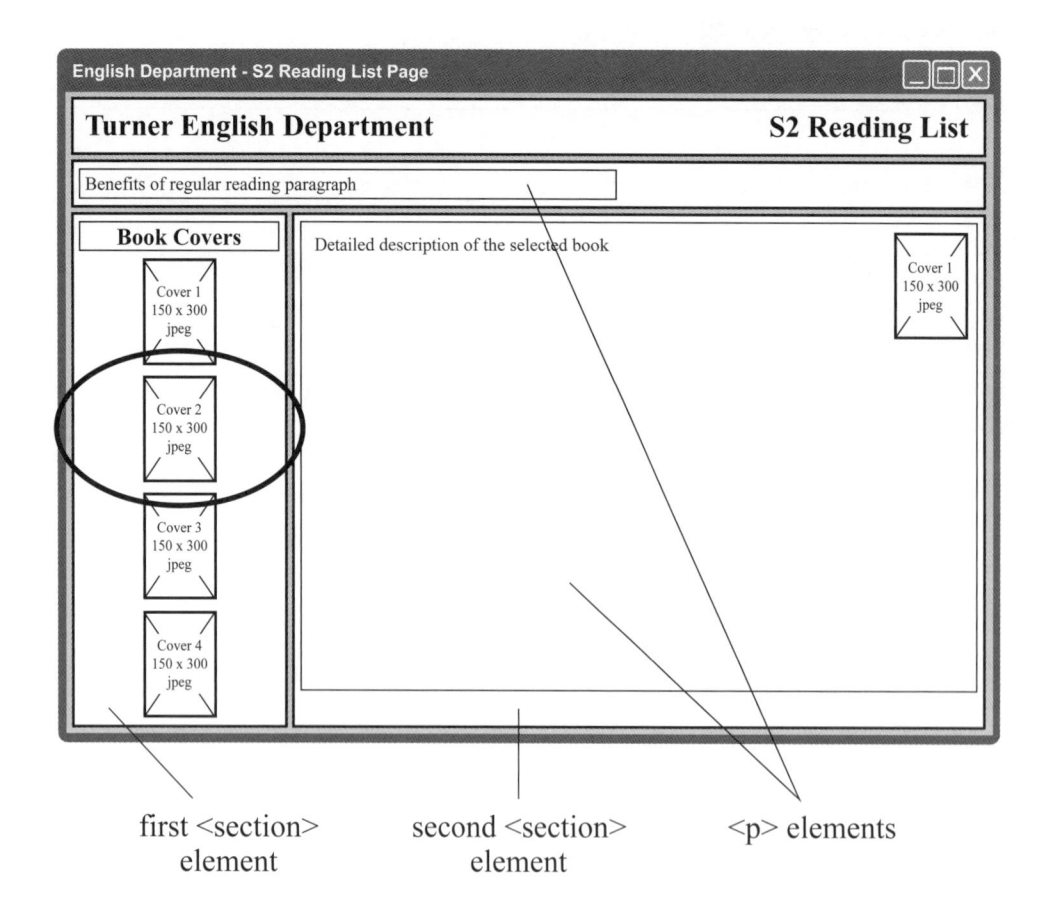

Cover 1 150 x 300 jpeg
Cover 2 150 x 300 jpeg (circled)
Cover 3 150 x 300 jpeg
Cover 4 150 x 300 jpeg

Cover 1 150 x 300 jpeg

first <section> element   second <section> element   <p> elements

Part of the HTML and JavaScript code from the web page is shown below:

```
...
<img class="coverImage" src="cover2.jpg" onclick="displayBook2()">
...
<script>
...
function displayBook2() {
document.getElementById("bookDescription1").style.display="none";
document.getElementById("bookDescription2").style.display="block";
document.getElementById("bookDescription3").style.display="none";
document.getElementById("bookDescription4").style.display="none";
}
...
</script>
```

MARKS | DO NOT WRITE IN THIS MARGIN

19. (d) (continued)

(i) State the type of element that has the ID "bookDescription1". **1**

(ii) Describe the purpose of the JavaScript code shown above. **3**

(iii) One of the book descriptions contains Unicode characters.

State one advantage of using Unicode characters rather than ASCII characters in web pages. **1**

(e) The web page uses bit-mapped graphic files for the book covers.

State one advantage of using bit-mapped graphic files rather than vector graphic files on this web page. **1**

[Turn over

20. A science department has 120 candidates taking courses in biology, chemistry and physics. The school wishes to identify how many candidates gained a grade 'A' in all three sciences and to save their names to a separate file.

An extract of the data is shown below:

...
Ann Smith,A,B,B
Peter Irwin,B,C,A
Dan Wu,B,B,C
Stacey Williams,A,A,A
Callum Reid,A,F,B
Kevin Richardson,A,A,A
...

The top-level design for the program is shown below.

1. Get details from file
2. Find and count names of students with three As
3. Display number of students with three As
4. Save three As in file

(a) Complete the table below to show the data flow in and out of steps 2 and 3. **4**

Step	In/out	Data flow
1	IN	
	OUT	name(), bio(), che(), phy()
2	IN	
	OUT	
3	IN	
	OUT	
4	IN	threeA()
	OUT	

20. (continued)

(b) Using a recognised design technique, refine step 2.

5

[Turn over

20. (continued)

(c) Using a recognised design technique, refine step 4. **4**

(d) The program is modular and uses procedures.

Describe one benefit of designing a modular solution to this program. **1**

[END OF SPECIMEN QUESTION PAPER]

ADDITIONAL SPACE FOR ANSWERS

ADDITIONAL SPACE FOR ANSWERS

HIGHER
Answers

ANSWERS FOR
SQA HIGHER COMPUTING SCIENCE 2018

HIGHER COMPUTING SCIENCE 2017

Section 1

Question		Expected Answer(s)	Max mark
1.		−32,768 to +32,767 OR -2^{16-1} to $(2^{16-1}) - 1$	2

2.		• Requirements elicitation e.g.
		  ○ Interview Client
		  ○ Inspect documentation
		  ○ Observation
		• Produce(software) specification
		• Identify inputs/processes/outputs
		• Identify scope/boundaries
		• Functional requirements detailing features of software
			2

3.		96000 × 16 × 120 × 2 = 368 640 000/8 = 46 080 000/1024 = 45 000/1024 = 43·9 Mb	3
4.		A compound key is a key field made up of two or more fields (that are primary keys in other tables/foreign keys) A surrogate key is created to introduce a primary key (in the absence of a natural primary key)	2
5.		Unauthorised access to personal data (sent to third parties through the tracking cookie)	1
6.		• A public key is used to encrypt the personal data • A private key is used to decrypt the personal data	2
7.	(a)	• High resolution displays • High-contrast themes • Icons supplemented with auditory feedback • Screen magnifying software • Screen reader software • Speech recognition software • Braille display/keyboard • Appropriate colour schemes	1
	(b)	• Subtitles/closed caption/text transcript • Replace system sounds like beeps with visual notifications and captioned text • Use visual warnings, such as a blinking title bar or a flashing border, whenever the computer generates a sound • (Noise cancelling) headphones	1

Question		Expected Answer(s)	Max mark
8.		• Uses classes/sub-classes • Classes are created with attributes and methods • Subclasses inherit code of a superclass • Objects of these classes can be instantiated • Methods perform an operation • Attributes store properties/values (for an instance) • Subclasses need only define additional attributes and methods	2
9.	(a)	RECORD BookDetails IS {STRING title, STRING author, INTEGER number of pages, REAL price}	2
	(b)	Create variable ListOfBooks [999] of (data type) BookDetails OR DECLARE ListOfBooks AS ARRAY OF BookDetails INITIALLY [] * 999	2

Section 2

Question		Expected Answer(s)	Max mark

10.	(a)	SET minpos TO 0
		SET minimum TO temps(0)
		FOR index FROM 1 TO 23 DO
		  IF temps (index) < minimum THEN
		    SET minpos TO index
		    SET minimum TO temps (index)
		  END IF
		NEXT index
		SEND " The... was" & minimum & "Celsius..." at hour" & index
		OPEN "low.txt"
		SEND minimum TO FILE
		Close "low.txt"
		
		SET minpos TO 0
		FOR index FROM 1 TO 23 DO
		  IF temps (index) < temps(minpos) THEN
		    SET minpos TO index
		  END IF
		NEXT index
		SEND " The... was" & temps(minpos) & "Celsius..." at hour" & minpos
		OPEN "low.txt"
		SEND temps(minpos) TO FILE
		Close "low.txt"
			7

Question			Expected Answer(s)	Max mark

	(b)		File management:
			  ○ identifies a free space on backing storage to place file
			  OR
			  ○ updates/checks file directory
			• Memory management:
			  ○ locates data in main memory
			  OR
			  ○ allocates main memory for process
			• Input/Output:
			  ○ transfer from memory to backing storage
			• Resource allocation:
			  ○ managing processes and memory
				2

	(c)	(i)	Iteration / Total / Average 2 / 18 / 9 3 / 30 / 10	2
		(ii)	Calculation results in the wrong data type i.e. real for the variable average Make average a real variable	2
	(d)		• Change the number 23 to END OF LIST • Use a conditional loop that utilises END OF LIST/FILE as a condition • Use a function to determine the size of the array • Accept a parameter that is used to define the size of the array	1
	(e)		• Remote access to control heating when not at home • Use of geolocation can automatically turn heating off when no one is home • Takes account of external weather forecast and adjusts temperature accordingly • Real time temperature monitoring through mobile devices can reduce unnecessary gas/fuel use • Data can be analysed to determine how quickly a home heats and how slowly it loses heat meaning that the boiler can be used more efficiently • Multi-room control systems prevent rooms being overheated when not in use	2
11.	(a)		Customer → Booking → Driver → Car	3
	(b)	(i)	Customer.Known As Booking.Booking ID Booking.From Booking.To Booking.Cost Car.Registration OR Driver.Registration	3
		(ii)	(Booking.)Booking ID=12345	1
	(c)		• The onmouseover event is triggered • Executing the mouseOver function • Changing the (style) colour to yellow(of the phrase "Welcome to Super Taxi"/heading)	2

Question		Expected Answer(s)	Max mark
	(d)	<meta name="keywords" content="super,taxi,…..">	2

	(e)	Search (index) for key words in
		  ○ title tags
		  ○ alt tags
		  ○ body/page/content
		  ○ URL
		• Checking links to the site from other sites
		• Data analytics e.g. hit rate, location by proximity, filters, prominent social media presence
		• Algorithms to determine relevance
			2

	(f)	Head section of the HTML	1
	(g)	• External more efficient as loaded once/cached but used by several pages • Internal loaded every time a page is accessed	2
12.	(a)	• Arrival OR • Departure Any one bullet from: • A formal parameter can be a copy of the actual parameter • A formal parameter can be a pointer/placeholder to the actual parameter • A formal parameter can control the flow of data e.g. by reference or by value	2
	(b)	The values are switched/passed into the incorrect parameters 10 – 13 results in –3 hours_parked is less than 1	2
	(c)	Watchpoints are used to stop execution when the value of a specific variable changes/pre-determined conditions are met This allows the programmer to compare the value with the expected value	2
	(d)	• More efficient as memory assigned to a local variable becomes available once function is terminated • Allows variables of the same name in different modules without affecting others • Aids modularity	2
13.	(a)	• Users given task/scenario to perform on the software • Suitable target set of users e.g. novice, experienced • Observation of performance of users • Feedback is given to developers	2
	(b)	• Sort by • Your basket • Page styles/(Gallery/List View) • Buttons: Buy; Pre Order; View Selection; View All • "i" icon (next to pre-order)	1

ANSWERS FOR HIGHER COMPUTING SCIENCE

Question			Expected Answer(s)	Max mark
	(c)		• Connection with server/database established OR reference to PHP/server-side scripting • Data captured on webpage form is used to construct a query • A query is used to check number of available items and release date • The result of the query is processed/returned (to update the webpage)	3
	(d)	(i)	Description of backup with frequency e.g. • Back up all data/(full back up) weekly/daily • Save changes since last full backup (differential) daily/hourly • Saving changes since last back up of any type (incremental) daily/hourly Backup type name and frequency	2
		(ii)	Cloud Offline Off-site repository Distributed storage Mirror disk Full/incremental/differential (not mentioned in part (i))	1
	(e)		• All text in correct colours: "Welcome To" and "Glasgow" would be displayed in red; "PC Bits" in blue • Alignment & size: all text centred, PC Bits double size/200% Welcome To **PCBits** Glasgow	2
14.	(a)		• Public cloud does not mean open access • Password protected space is rented to public • Data may be encrypted • Data protected by firewall	2
	(b)	(i)	Vector as: • You can drag individual objects without affecting others • Ear could be grouped as a set of objects • Objects can be layered • Attributes/co-ordinates of ears can be changed	2
		(ii)	• Vector increases • Bitmap stays the same	2

Question			Expected Answer(s)	Max mark
15.	(a)		• Address of instruction placed on address bus • Read line (on control bus) is activated • Contents of location (instruction) transferred to a register along data bus • Instruction decoded/executed	3
	(b)	(i)	• Stores frequently accessed instructions/data • Faster access times than main memory • Fewer accesses to slower main memory • On the same chip as the processor • Cache is static RAM (faster)	2
		(ii)	• Instructions 2/3 will already be (pre-loaded) in cache i.e. a cache hit will occur • Data in location 2000 will already be in cache improving access time/instruction time.	2
	(c)		16777216 colours is better than 65536	2
	(d)	(i)	• Interframe saves the differences between frames • Intraframe compresses a single frame (using RLE or 'blocking' shades of colours)	2
		(ii)	• More effective compression for a singer performer • (Differential/delta/i/p) Interframes will be smaller for a performance with fewer movements • (Differential/delta/i/p) Interframes will be larger for performance with more movement • More key/delta frames will be needed as dancers will be moving around	2

HIGHER COMPUTING SCIENCE 2018

Section 1

Question	Expected Answer(s)	Max mark
1.	1000 1000	1
2.	• A public key is used to encrypt the personal data **(1 mark)** • A private key is used to decrypt the personal data **(1 mark)** **OR** • Public key is known to all systems **(1 mark)** • Private key to one system only **(1 mark)**	2
3.	Rules **(1 mark)** 1 mark for any one bullet from • Use variables which can be applied to existing fact/rules • Reduces the need for repetition of facts/additional lines of code • Adds information/meaning based on other facts/rules • Establishes relationships between facts/rules • Can implement recursion **OR** Queries **(1 mark)** • allow facts/rules to be interrogated **(1 mark)** **OR** Pattern matching **(1 mark)** • allows facts/rules to be matched. **(1 mark)**	2
4.	• Malware on one drive automatically mirrored on backup • Corruption and accidental deletion of original data mirrored on backup • Additional cost of duplicated hard drive • Higher energy consumption as a result of writing to multiple disks at the same time	2
5.	Unicode can represent more characters **(1 mark)** 1 mark for any one bullet from • 2^{16} when compared to ASCII $2^8/2^7$ **OR** • uses 16 bits compared to 8/7 *Also acceptable:* • UTF-8, UTF-16, UTF-32 or UCS-2 • (17×2^{16})	2
6.	A key added to an entity to act as a primary/unique key **(1 mark)** 1 mark for any one from • Where no natural (primary) key already exists • Surrogate key does not add meaning to the entity	2

Question	Expected Answer(s)	Max mark
7. (a)	Line 8: position to index **(1 mark)** Line 10: 1 mark for any bullet • target=list(position) • target = list(index) • position = index	2
(b)	−1	1
8.	Read line (on control bus) is activated **(1 mark)** Instruction is transferred (from memory) to the processor on the data bus **(1 mark)**	2
9. (a)	• Multi-core/number of processors • Increase width of data bus • Increase clock speed • Increase RAM/memory • Increase use of solid state • Any other valid response	1
(b)	Matching reason e.g. • Simultaneous execution of instructions/parallel processing • More bits transferred in a single operation • More fetch-executes per clock pulse • Reduces the need/faster access to access slower backing storage • Faster access than slower backing storage	1
10. (a)	• Version of/out of date operating system • Downloaded file is corrupt	1
(b)	• Insufficient amount of RAM/memory • Minimum clock speed not available • Version of processor • Version of graphics card	1

Section 2

Question	Expected Answer(s)	Max mark
11. (a) (i)	• Public cloud services can be easily increased or decreased to match current needs • Can set up or easily expand capacity of public cloud storage without (Securebell) purchasing hardware • Public cloud removes need for backup/maintenance/administration strategies (for SecureBell) • Public cloud has lower initial costs than private cloud *Also acceptable:* • The converse of each if private cloud is referenced.	2
(ii)	• Username **and** passwords to access public cloud • Use of encryption • Firewall • Require use of digital certificate	2

ANSWERS FOR HIGHER COMPUTING SCIENCE

Question			Expected Answer(s)	Max mark
	(b)		• Must provide keys for decryption (when approved access is required) • Provide facilities for public authorities (e.g. police/MI5 government) to access electronic communications • Provide hardware and software to facilitate surveillance of electronic communications • Pay for the hardware needed to store electronic communication • Inform staff that access to communication data is subject to RIPA	2
	(c)	(i)	33 177 600 (bits) **(2 marks)** OR • Bit depth: 16 **(1 mark)** • 33 177 600 (bits) **(1 mark)** *Also acceptable*: • Bit depth of 2 (bytes) **(1 mark)**	2
		(ii)	• Key frames/I-frames are stored **(1 mark)** • Saves changes between (key) frames **(1 mark)**	2
	(d)	(i)	Bitmap **(1 mark)** 1 mark for any one from • Image has become pixelated • Image is resolution dependent	2
		(ii)	• Stores the colour of a pixel **(1 mark)** • and the number of repetitions of that colour **(1 mark)**	2
12.	(a)		• Create prototypes/wireframes/ design of user interface • Prospective users perform tasks • Developers observe/interview/ discuss scenarios with users • Obtain feedback to influence changes	3
	(b)	(i)	Record name and appropriate start/end e.g. { } **(1 mark)** Four fields with correct data types **(1 mark)** *E.g.* `RECORD movie IS { STRING title, STRING studio, INTEGER rating, REAL takings }`	2
		(ii)	Array of 100 **(1 mark)** Data type matching answer in (a) **(1 mark)** *E.g.* `DECLARE topMovies AS ARRAY OF movie INITIALLY[]*99`	2

Question		Expected Answer(s)	Max mark

	(c)	Initialise and increment count **(1 mark)**
		Loop that traverses array **(1 mark)**
		If condition with:
		• correct use of array variable **(1 mark)**
		• comparing current value of studio field to target **(1 mark)**
		Open/Create & Close <u>file</u> **(1 mark)**
		Write target & count to file **(1 mark)**
		E.g.
		`DECLARE count INITIALLY 0`
		`RECEIVE target FROM KEYBOARD`
		`FOR index FROM 0 TO 99 DO`
		`  IF topMovies(index).studio`
		`  = target`
		`    THEN`
		`       count=count+1`
		`  END IF`
		`END FOR`
		`OPEN "highest.txt"`
		`  WRITE target, count`
		`CLOSE "highest.txt"`
			6

13.	(a)	• Database (holding city data) is not stored locally • Database must be accessed/queried from (remote) server • Client (browser) cannot access database directly	1
	(b) (i)	H1 with open and close bracket **(1 mark)** AND <u>Any two</u> from three correct elements with appropriate attribute for 1 mark each **(maximum 2 marks)**	3
	(ii)	• Use external style sheet/create a file with CSS rules • Create a link tag to external stylesheet • Place link to external stylesheet in all web pages	2
	(c)	• Normal(this) **(1 mark)** • x.style.height = "96px"; **(1 mark)** 1 mark for <u>both</u> bullets: • x.style.height = "32px" • x.style.width = "32px";	3
	(d)	• Text in form assigned to variables • Connection with server/database established • Database <u>selected</u> • (Form data used to) construct (SQL) query/query is run • Results of query returned <u>from server.</u> • Code (PHP) processes result to generate appropriate output.	4

104 ANSWERS FOR HIGHER COMPUTING SCIENCE

Question		Expected Answer(s)	Max mark
14.	(a)	Customer ← Lesson → Instructor → Resort *1 mark for each correct relationship*	3
	(b)	InstructorID and StartTime and Date	1
	(c)	Lesson.StartTime Lesson.Date Lesson.InstructorID Instructor.FirstName Customer.FirstName Customer.Surname *1 mark for the three correct tables* *1 mark for the six correct fields* *1 mark for relating fields to correct tables* *Also acceptable*: • Instructor.InstructorID	3
	(d)	[Lesson.Date]=17/12/18 **(1 mark)** (AND) [Lesson.InstructorID] = 14 **(1 mark)** *Also acceptable*: • [Instructor.InstructorID] • Valid alternative date formats	2
	(e)	• Summary Field • Report Footer	1
	(f)	• Cost of additional servers or cloud storage • Subscription costs associated with software licenses for server-side software • Cost of connecting servers to ISPs • Cost of employing/training additional staff	1
	(g)	• Connect with others interested in skiing • Exposure to people of a different demographic • Sharing ideas/reviews of ski resorts and instructors	1
15.	(a)	• The upper index of the array is one less than the length of the array • Upper − 1 is the highest index position of the array • (Exceeds array index) so runtime error would occur	1
	(b)	heat1 is the actual parameter **(1 mark)** list is the formal parameter **(1 mark)** 1 mark for any one bullet from • Formal parameter (list) contains the pointer/address of actual parameter (heat 1) • Any changes to the formal parameter (list) are automatically made to the actual parameter	3

Question		Expected Answer(s)	Max mark
	(c)	• Local OR lines 1/2 to lines 9/10 **(1 mark)** • It is only used within the function in which it is declared **(1 mark)**	2
	(d)	A = 13.4 B = 14.5 C = 17.4	3
	(e) (i)	• Use of < (instead of >) • On line 5, list(index) and min should swap places	1
	(ii)	Logic	1
	(iii)	• The maximum time/16.4 in heat 2 is lower than the maximum time/17.4 in heat 1 **(1 mark)** • which coincides with the fastest time/10.1 being in heat 2 **(1 mark)**	2
	(f) (i)	• (If the times are equal) the IF condition is false/not met/is not less than **(1 mark)** • therefore the else statement is executed **(1 mark)**	2
	(ii)	Concept of nested if or else if statement	1
	(g)	• Tracks/checks available memory • Allocates space/addresses in RAM for the function • Protects other processes	2

ANSWERS FOR HIGHER COMPUTING SCIENCE

HIGHER COMPUTING SCIENCE
2018 SPECIMEN QUESTION PAPER

Section 1

Question			Expected Answer(s)	Max mark
1.			−277	1
2.			Either one from: • It is harder to manage the project when you cannot meet the client regularly • The agile methodology requires more client interaction throughout the whole project, than the iterative one does	1
3.			Award 1 mark each for: • Slow performance • Inability to access data	2
4.			Award 1 mark for each correct row | category | Most expensive item | |---|---| | A | 6.99 | | B | 2.99 |	2
5.			Either one from: • Accidental use of the same variable in different modules • It may be difficult for more than one programmer to work on the code	1
6.	(a)	(i)	To find and store the time for the first instance the chosen player completed the game	1
		(ii)	To find the other times the chosen player completed the game and continually store their fastest time (find minimum)	1
	(b)		An end-of-file error will occur	1

7.			Award 1 mark each for:
			• onmouseclick
			• Width and height 300 pixels
			• Function created
			
			`<img src="guitar.jpg" onmouseclick="displayBig(this)">`
			
			`<script>`
			`  function displayBig(my_image)`
			`  {my_image.style.width='300px';`
			`  my_image.style.height='300px';}`
			`</script>`
				3

8.			Award 1 mark each for: • Showing each president to one club • Showing each club to one or more members For example: [diagram: president 1–4 mapped to club 1–4, mapped to member 1–5]	2

Question		Expected Answer(s)	Max mark
9.		Mantissa sign bit = 0 Mantissa magnitude = 101 1000 0000 0000 Exponent = 1111 1110 0101 1000 0000 0000 1111 1110 Award 1 mark each for: • Sign bit — 0 • Mantissa — 1011 0000 0000 000 • Exponent (two's complement) — 1111 1110 Additional guidance: $0.001011 = 0.1011 \times 2^{-2}$	3
10.		Either one from: • Navigation bars • User inputs Additional acceptable answers: • Hyperlinks • Input types (including radio buttons, text box)	1
11.	(a)	Either one from: • Increased cache memory • Faster cache memory Additional acceptable answers: • Faster memory bus speed	1
	(b)	The greater the bus width, the more bits can be fetched (1 mark) in a single operation (1 mark)	2
12.		Award 1 mark each for: • A public key is used to encrypt data • A private key is used to decrypt data	2
13.		It allows missing links and/or orphan links to be found	1

Section 2

Question			Expected Answer(s)	Max mark
14.	(a)		Award 1 mark each for: • tournamentID in Entry • playerID in Entry	2
	(b)		Award 1 mark for each row from: | Field(s) and calculation(s) | Maximum Prize Money for First = MAX(prizeMoney) | |---|---| | Table(s) and query | [All entries for Sue Pollock] | | Search criteria | position = 1 | | Grouping | | | Sort order | |	3
	(c)	(i)	So that each country only appears once	1
		(ii)	Award 1 mark each for: • (AS) [Over 7000] is missing from SQL • The second half of JOIN should be = Entry.tournamentID	2
	(d)		SELECT SUM (1 mark) (prizemoney*0.1) (1 mark) AS [Retained prize money](1 mark) FROM Result;	3

Question			Expected Answer(s)	Max mark
	(e)		Award 1 mark each for: • Cardinality — one club to many players • Relationship — player is "member of" a club or similar	2
15.	(a)		Award 1 mark each for: • First level including box to represent navigation bar: residential property and commercial property • Second level linked from each department: renting and buying with correct links	2

	(b)		Award 1 mark for each line of code:
			`header, nav, main {margin-top:5px; margin-bottom:5px; padding:10px}`
			`footer, section {padding:5px}`
			`footer {margin-top:5px}`
			`section {margin-left:10px; margin-top:10px}`
				4

	(c)	(i)	Award 1 mark each for: • Length • Presence	2
		(ii)	7	1
		(iii)	The change would mean that all property types would be restricted to a maximum of 3 months and therefore the form would not be fit for its intended purpose	1
	(d)	(i)	Award 1 mark each for: • Using different devices • Using different browsers	2
		(ii)	Personas: a type of user with a specific age and experience Test cases: a set of actions to verify a particular feature or function	2
16.	(a)		Either one from: • Message • shiftLettersBy	1
	(b)		Award 1 mark for each row | Break in execution	character	newMessage
---	---	---
First	c	f
Second	a	fd
Third	b	fde		3

Question			Expected Answer(s)	Max mark
	(c)	(i)	This will be a pre-defined function to change ASCII to character In the majority of languages this will be ORD	1
		(ii)	This will be a pre-defined function to change ASCII to character In the majority of languages this will be CHR	1
	(d)		The shiftLetterBy value entered may take the character beyond the bounds of ASCII values (0-255)	1
	(e)		Award 1 mark each for: • Loop for each character • Extract next character • Concatenate onto new message Pseudocode example answer: 1. Initialise newMessage 2. Start fixed loop for each character 3. Extract next character from message 4. Add next character to the front of newMessage 5. End fixed loop Structure diagram example answer:	3
17.	(a)		Award 1 mark each for any two valid answers. For example: • Database should store every race/team/driver from 1950 to most recent • Database should be searchable for number of team wins • Database should be searchable for number of driver wins • Database should be searchable for a team's results over the years • Database should be searchable for a driver's results over the years • Database should be sortable to find most and least successful team in order Award 1 mark for any unlisted but valid answer	2
	(b)		Award 1 mark each for any three from: • Cardinality of Team — Driver (should be one-to-many) • No unique identifier in the Race entity • Car number can't be a unique field, as it is allocated each year • noOFWins is not required, as this can be calculated from position	3

… ANSWERS FOR HIGHER COMPUTING SCIENCE   107

Question			Expected Answer(s)	Max mark
	(c)	(i)	Award 1 mark for each correct entry | country	championshipWins
---	---
Austria	4
France	3
Germany	6
India	0
Italy	21
UK	28		2
		(ii)	Award 1 mark for each correct row | Field(s) and calculation(s)	teamName
---	---
Table(s)	Team
Search criteria	dateFounded = _ _/_ _/195_
Grouping	
Sort order			2
18.	(a)	(i)	Award 1 mark each for: • Record declaration • Five variables • Correct data type for variables SQA Reference Language example answer: `RECORD participant IS {STRING idNumber, STRING firstname, STRING, lastname, STRING town, INTEGER score}`	3
		(ii)	Award 1 mark each for: • Array • Of 5000 records SQA Reference Language example answer: `DECLARE participants AS array of participant * 5000 INITIALLY[]`	2

	(b)		Award 1 mark each for:
			• Set highposition to first position
			• Fixed loop: 1 TO 4999
			• Condition: check current score is greater than score at current highest position
			• Store new position if condition true
			
			SQA Reference Language example answer:
			`SET highposition TO 0`
			`FOR loop FROM 1 TO 4999 DO`
			`IF participants[loop].score > participants[highposition].score THEN`
			`  SET highposition TO loop`
			`END IF`
			`NEXT`
				4

	(c)		Award 1 mark each for any two from: • Unauthorised access to computer material • Unauthorised access with intent to commit a further offence • Unauthorised modification of data on a computer	2

Question			Expected Answer(s)	Max mark
19.	(a)		Award 1 mark each for any two from: • No navigation • Too much information for a smart phone screen • Landscape design does not suit smartphone use	2
	(b)		Award 1 mark each for: • To position the two <h1> headings either side of the page • To position the two <section> elements side-by-side	2
	(c)		Award 1 mark each for: • White background • Dark green text colour • Fits the width of the section • Text is 10px in from the edge of the paragraph element boundary and an additional 5px from the top of the section	4
	(d)	(i)	<p> OR Paragraph	1
		(ii)	Award 1 mark each for: • When the book cover is clicked, the function is called • It shows one of four paragraphs • While hiding the other three	3
		(iii)	More characters can be represented	1
	(e)		They produce more realistic photographic images	1
20.	(a)			4

Module	In/out	Data flow	
2	IN	bio(), che(), phy(), name()	1 mark
	OUT	total threeA()	1 mark 1 mark
3	IN	total	1 mark
	OUT		

| | (b) | | Award 1 mark each for:
• Initialise total
• Use of fixed loop (120 times)
• Complex selection statement (all three subjects = A)
• Incrementing total
• Store three A candidate names

Pseudocode example answer:
1. Initialise total to 0
2. Start fixed loop for 120 candidates
3.   If biologyMark = A and chemistryMark = A and physicsMark = A
4.   Increment total
5.   Store candidate name
6.   End if
7. End fixed loop | 5 |

Question		Expected Answer(s)	Max mark

	(b)	Structure diagram example answer:
		
		- store numbers of students with three As and the names of those students
		  - initialise total to 0
		  - initialise names to empty list
		  - loop for 120 students
		    - If biology mark = A and chemistry mark = A and physics mark = A
		      - yes
		        - increment total
		        - store student's name
			5

	(c)	Award 1 mark each for: • Creating a file • Fixed loop for number of three A candidates • Writing threeA names to file • Closing file Pseudocode example answer: 1. Create Science File 2. Start fixed loop for number of Three "A" candidates 3. write candidate names to file 4. End fixed loop 5. Close file	4
	(d)	Award 1 mark for any one from: • Different programmers can implement different parts of the design • Each part of the design can be tested separately when implemented • Design shows main processes	1

Acknowledgements

Permission has been sought from all relevant copyright holders and Hodder Gibson is grateful for the use of the following:

Image © Anastasiia Makarova/Shutterstock.com (2018 page 8).